Eugene Grissom

A Statement to the Friends of the N.C. Insane Asylum

Eugene Grissom

A Statement to the Friends of the N.C. Insane Asylum

ISBN/EAN: 9783337370633

Printed in Europe, USA, Canada, Australia, Japan

Cover: Foto ©ninafisch / pixelio.de

More available books at **www.hansebooks.com**

A STATEMENT

TO

THE FRIENDS

OF THE

INSANE ASYLUM.

RALEIGH:
E. M. UZZELL, STEAM PRINTER AND BINDER.
1889.

A STATEMENT

TO

THE FRIENDS

OF THE

INSANE ASYLUM.

RALEIGH:
E. M. UZZELL, STEAM PRINTER AND BINDER.
1889.

TO THE FRIENDS

OF THE

North Carolina Insane Asylum.

In view of the labored efforts which have been made to discredit the decision of the Board of Directors of this institution in the recent investigation of charges against its Superintendent; in behalf of the fair fame of the noblest public charity of your fathers, and in simple justice to the Board and myself, I wish to lay before you the facts from the records of the institution, and the evidence in this trial, and ask your candid consideration.

OF THE HISTORY OF THESE CHARITIES.

The history of asylums for the insane teaches the same lesson everywhere: that they must have the welfare of the patients as the sole object of their existence. So far as other motives have operated in asylum government, however expedient in their proper sphere, they have only embarrassed the operations, and sometimes fatally injured the work, of charity and humanity. The causes of success or failure, in an undertaking of such responsibility, were deeply pondered by me when called to the task of the superintendence of the North Carolina Insane Asylum.

No institution of the kind that had been used as the stepping-stone of political elevation, or as the foot-ball of partisan strife, had ever attained a high standard of respectability or usefulness. The paramount interests involved were the comfort and care of the unfortunate and the welfare of the State, and from the moment of my election I determined to know no other guides in my official course, and I have faithfully maintained that resolution.

It is true that on account of the interest I had taken in the political movements of the State, in my earlier years, it was not surprising that the fear should be entertained and expressed by some that a partisan spirit would affect my official action in the discharge of the delicate and responsible duties devolving upon the Superintendent. But this misgiving was so thoroughly dispelled in the minds of those most intimately acquainted with the conduct of its affairs that, as will be seen, within three years after I was sustained and generously upheld by a Democratic Board which had replaced the original Republican body to which I owed my first election.

THE CIRCUMSTANCES OF MY ELECTION.

The reconstruction acts of Congress and the Constitution of North Carolina adopted thereunder vacated every office, executive, judicial and ministerial, from Governor to trustees and directors of the several State institutions. Although the existing *personnel* was thus destroyed, yet the organic law of the Insane Asylum remained, and no change was made in the existing statutes pertaining thereto. A new Board was appointed for the management of the institution under the pre-existing law.

When the organization took place Dr. E. C. Fisher, the old Superintendent, was not a candidate for the position, but Dr. Fleming, of the United States Army, was, and in the course of the election the choice of the Board fell upon myself.

Dr. Fleming then asked for the position of Assistant Physician, but at my especial and earnest request, Dr. F. T. Fuller, who had occupied the position from the earliest days of the institution, was retained, and has been continuously re-elected ever since.

To those acquainted with the history of my administration of the Asylum, always with the end in view that, it is hoped, has been successfully attained, it would seem preposterous that the Superintendent should have had to meet any charge of partisanship or mismanagement, personal or official.

INAUGURATION OF A NON-PARTISAN POLICY.

Upon assuming the duties of the office, July 17th, 1868, I found the employees of the institution in a state of consternation from the fear of wholesale discharge.

I announced at once that no employee should be removed for any political reason, or through any political influence, so far as I could prevent it. This assurance quieted the existing perturbation and was effectual in retaining the corps of attendants and employees. It was not long before they recognized that character and efficiency were the only considerations involved in their retention or promotion, and steady improvement was discernible. I also respectfully requested the Board of Directors to re-elect the Steward, Mr. James H. Moore, and the Treasurer, Colonel William E. Anderson, both of whom had made efficient officers, as I had been informed.

The Board, however, elected Messrs. E. A. Whitaker, Steward, and Charles H. Horner, Treasurer. At the expiration of their terms, through my earnest solicitation, the two old officers, Messrs. Moore and Anderson, were reinstated by the same Board that had elected me. From the beginning to the present day the whole course of my policy has been directed to the elevation of this great charity above party influences, and to maintain for it the dignity enjoyed by institutions of a similar character in other States. The entire administration and conduct of the institution for over twenty years has been managed upon a strictly humanitarian basis, above the motives and ends of partisan action. The delicate duties devolving upon medical officers and attendants, requiring experience, tact, patience, foresight, watchfulness, and, indeed, a life of sympathy and devotion to duty, set this work conspicuously apart from the arena of political strife, and demanded for it the sole consecration of the life and ambition of him who would fulfill the allotted task.

EMINENT MEN OF THE DEMOCRATIC BOARD OF 1871.

The responsibility involving the fate of so many unfortunate human beings, many of them eminent in the various walks of life, before falling victims to disease, has been profoundly appreciated by our wise and prudent citizens in the several Boards of Directors for many years past. Upon a change in political power, in 1870, the board that elected me was removed and the following gentlemen took charge of the institution: Dr. Charles E. Johnson, Dr. E. Burke Haywood, Charles Dewey, Esq., P. F. Pescud, Sr., Esq., Hon. A. S. Merrimon, Hon. Kemp P. Battle, Dr. C. T. Murphy, Dr. John McCormick, Rev. Dr. B. Craven, Dr. J. J. Summerell, Hon. Thomas Bragg, Major C. Dowd, Dr. Pride Jones, and the Hon. Joseph J. Davis. Subsequently the Hon. W. N. H. Smith succeeded Governor Thomas Bragg. By this Board, so eminent in the councils of the State, I was retained, and the plans for the restoration and improvement of the institution from its condition of apparent neglect and imminent decay were cheerfully approved and sustained.

NEW BOARDS IN RAPID SUCCESSION.

The Board of 1871, organized upon legislative appointment, was displaced upon judicial sanction of the right of executive appointments in the several boards of the State institutions, and a Republican Board took its place in February, 1873, and was replaced in turn by a Democratic board, appointed by Governor Vance, upon his accession as Governor, in 1877. Of this body Dr. E. Burke Haywood was President, and it contained such men as J. M. Pool, Esq., Dr. B. F. Arrington, Col. James G. Burr, Dr. J. T. Leach, Rev. Dr. B. Craven, Major C. Dowd, Col. James S. Amis, Dr. S. G. Ward, and men equally known for their fidelity to the State and to the claims and needs of suffering humanity.

THE MISLEADING SPIRIT OF MALICIOUS FALSEHOOD.

It is now charged that I escaped being displaced by the Board of 1877 through the evasive trick of resigning an unexpired term in November, 1876, to secure re-election for a full term while the old Board of the Caldwell-Brogden administration was yet in power. How untruthful is this statement! The proceedings of the Board of Directors show that my term of office expired in 1876, and that the time for re-election had arrived when the Board met in annual session, November 1, 1876.

I quote from the record:

"At the regular annual meeting of the Board of Directors of the Insane Asylum, held at the institution on Wednesday, November 1st, 1876, at 10:30 o'clock A. M., the following members were present, viz.: Dr. J. G. Ramsay, D. R. Hardin, Esq., Col. G. W. Stanton, Col. W. R. Myers, Capt. C. H. Thomas, Dr. E. Burke Haywood, J. M. Pool, Esq., Anderson Betts, Esq., Col. T. G. Walton, Maj. F. H. Cameron, J. T. Pearson, Esq., Gen. W. D. Jones, Dr. B. F. Arrington, and John R. Goode, Esq. * * * * * Dr. E. Burke Haywood then stated that the next business in order was the election of officers.

"The board then went into the election of officers. Dr. E. Burke Haywood then stated that he had known Dr. Grissom for a number of years and he was satisfied that he was the right man in the right place, and it afforded him pleasure to nominate him for re-election to the office of Superintendent. Gen. W. D. Jones seconded Dr. Haywood's motion. The Board then proceeded to vote, which resulted in Dr. Grissom's being unanimously elected Superintendent."

SURRENDER OF THREE YEARS TENURE.

The recorded proceedings of all the Boards of the Asylum abundantly prove that I have at all times stood ready to conform to all new enactments of law.

I quote again from the record:

"At the adjourned meeting of the Board of Directors of the Insane Asylum of North Carolina, held at the executive office at 7:30 o'clock P. M., March 6th, 1878, the following members were present, viz.: Dr. E. Burke Haywood, Mr. Julius Lewis, Mr. A. M. McPheeters, Dr. J. T. Leach, Col. J. S. Amis, Col. J. G. Burr, Major C. Dowd, Rev. Dr. B. Craven, and Dr. S. G. Ward. Dr. E. B. Haywood in the chair, the meeting was called to order and the following business transacted:

"The president stated that he had received some legal opinions from the Governor (Vance) and requested Col. J. S. Amis to read them to the Board. Col. J. S. Amis then stated that Dr. Grissom had some legal opinions which he wished to lay before the Board. The chair then requested Major C. Dowd to read to the Board the legal opinions offered by Dr. Grissom. Major C.

Dowd then moved that all the legal opinions be accepted for consideration and discussion. Carried. After different members had given their views in the premises and the subject had been fully and freely discussed, Mr. A. M. McPheeters offered the following resolution, which was amended by Col. J. S. Amis:

"'WHEREAS, There are conflicting legal opinions from the most eminent lawyers of this State as to the legality of the election of Dr. Grissom as Superintendent of the Asylum in 1876 for eight years from the 1st of January, 1887, and Dr. Eugene Grissom being present and agreeing and consenting to conform to the recent act limiting the term of office of Superintendent to four years, and that his term of office shall begin from 1st of January, 1878, and continue for four years; therefore,

"'*Resolved*, That on account of these considerations, Dr. E. Grissom be regarded and sustained as Superintendent for four years from 1st of January, 1878.'

"The Board then proceeded to vote, which resulted in the unanimous passage of the resolution as amended."

WAIVING MY TENURE OF OFFICE AGAIN.

The Legislature from time to time changed the law governing the Asylum, and in these various changes suggested legal conflict with the tenure of office of the Superintendent, fixed sometimes at eight, six, and even four years, and chosen accordingly for a fixed term, the rights under which no mere statute law could ever impair.

But I have never stood in the way of the wishes of the people, fairly expressed through their representatives in the General Assembly, nor sought to hinder or embarrass the Board of Directors in the discharge of their duties according to the public wish and command. So again in 1881, lacking still one year of filling out the curtailed term, of which I had surrendered three years to the Board of 1877–'78, as shown above, in order to meet the wishes of the Board and leave them free and unembarrassed under a new law, then in operation, I waived all my rights in the premises and vacated the office. I quote again from the records of the Board of Directors:

"NORTH CAROLINA INSANE ASYLUM,
"April 6, 1881.

"The Board of Directors of the North Carolina Insane Asylum met in regular quarterly session at the Asylum at eleven and half o'clock. This was the first meeting of the Directors appointed under an act for the better government of the North Carolina Insane Asylum, ratified March 5, 1881. There were present Dr. E. Burke Haywood, Hon. A. S. Merrimon, R. H. Smith, Esq., Maj. Jas. C. MacRae, A. J. Tomlinson, Esq., W. S. Mason, Esq., W. S. Battle, Esq., and W. S. Harris, Esq. * * * After some informal discussion upon the tenure of office of Superintendent, the subject was informally passed over, and the President announced that the election of officers was in order. * * * Upon motion of W. S. Mason, Esq., the following communication "A" was read by the clerk, and was accepted according to its legal effect, and ordered to be filed:

"*To the Directors of the North Carolina Insane Asylum:*

"I hereby waive my right to hold the office of Superintendent of the North Carolina Insane Asylum, and consent that the office is now vacant.

"Respectfully submitted,

"April 6, 1881. [Signed] "EUGENE GRISSOM."

"Upon motion of W. S. Mason, Esq., the resolution to consider the election of a Superintendent was rescinded, and on his further motion the question was taken up.

"Upon motion of Mr. Mason, Dr. Eugene Grissom was unanimously elected Superintendent of the North Carolina Insane Asylum for six years next ensuing."

At the annual meeting in March, 1887, at the expiration of said term of six years, the Board, then composed of Dr. E. Burke Haywood, Prof. John B. Burwell, Geo. H. Snow, Esq., R. H. Smith, Esq., Dr. T. D. Haigh, Capt. W. S. Harris, Col. J. S. Amis, Dr. John McCormick, and Dr. W. R. Capehart, unanimously re-elected Dr. Grissom for another term of six years. Through all these changes, notwithstanding the varying questions of the hour, and the heated conflicts of the day, the same sentiment of approval of the exclusion of the institution from the struggles of political life has always prevailed, and the policy of the Superintendent has been heartily and courageously sustained year after year in the effort to maintain the Asylum on a high basis as a curative hospital.

CONTINUED PROGRESS AND IMPROVEMENT.

Almost every report bears witness to the continued progress and improvement of the institution in a material point of view, and finally, as its legitimate result, to its greatly advanced comfort and means of cure, the decrease of sickness, the lowering of the death rate, and the increase of the percentage of recoveries.

Intelligent visitors from abroad have everywhere spoken in high terms of the general appearance of comfort, and the discipline and *morale* of the inmates and the entire institution. It is not, I trust, improper to state, what is strictly in accord with the facts of its history, that with my administration of the affairs of the Asylum its usefulness in every respect, including the condition of the buildings, comfort of the patients, discipline of the organization, increase of admissions, and every other essential of its operations, has been extended from year to year.

This is not only acknowledged by those in North Carolina who have had friends under my treatment, but by the official visitors who have had charge and oversight of the institution during various State administrations. This recognition has also been cordially given by the superintendents of other institutions, and alienists generally, in this country, as manifested by numerous letters on file or in the hands of the late President of the Board, as well as by the high official positions bestowed upon me by the American Association of Superintendents of the Insane.

LIFTED UP FROM ITS FORMER STATE.

Those who remember the condition of the institution when I took charge, in 1868, will bear witness that its standard was very low; both as to usefulness and comfort.

Whatever was the cause the facts remain that the wards themselves, the kitchen, cooking apparatus, means of serving food, water-works, heating apparatus, and all outside buildings were exceedingly defective and in a condition of general decline.

The building itself had not received a coat of paint in twelve years since its erection, the roof was in bad order, the ventilation was totally inadequate, the grounds encumbered with the original embankments of clay from the excavations for the foundation. The wards, and indeed the entire structure, were unsupplied with furniture proper for the comfort of inmates, even to the lack of sufficient bed clothing for the rigors of winter, nor were there any proper appliances for protection from fire. It is not necessary to enlarge upon a picture, ungrateful to recall, and only referred to in justice to the enlightened Boards that have judiciously and cordially co-operated in the gradual elevation of the Asylum to its proper place as a hospital.

INCREASE OF INMATES AND DECREASED DEATH RATE.

As a further evidence of the increased usefulness of the Asylum, in the fulfillment of the designs of its humane and patriotic founders, its statistics show that the number of patients has been regularly and constantly increased, except during the interval of the transfer of a certain number of inmates to the Western Insane Asylum at Morganton. The largest number ever under treatment up to 1868, at the period of my taking charge, was 217. This has been carefully and gradually increased to 292, an addition of more than one-third, and, I am thankful to add, with a corresponding increase of the cured and a decrease of the proportionate death rate.

The true object of effort in a curative hospital must be efficiency rather than simple economy, and yet, in view of the demands upon tax-payers, economy must also demand careful consideration. It is therefore with satisfaction that I add that all the improvements which have been mentioned, involving the conduct of the institution according to greatly enlarged ideas of personal accommodation and comfort of the patients, have been accomplished without any increase of expenditure *per capita*, as a comparison with the early records on file will show.

WHAT DID THE STATE DESIGN?

What did North Carolina intend to perform when this institution was organized? Was it to relieve the needs of the unhappy insane so far as its capacity would allow? Was it to seek to cure, as far as the resources of modern science are available, in this most serious and dreadful of maladies? Was it to alleviate the miseries of the sick and to limit the death rate as far as may be possible? Was it to lighten the burden of intolerable care and anxiety, and resulting poverty, illness, and re-produced insanity itself, in the stricken family circle? Was it to greatly reduce the number of helpless or of dangerous chronic insane lingering in poor-houses and jails to the great cost and horror of the community? Was it to win a high place in the regard of the intelligent and humane throughout the world as a noble and enlightened Commonwealth, standing side by side with the foremost of the earth in the most beneficent labors of humanity? If such were her objects, they have been achieved. Its statistics are among the proudest of the land. The Board of Directors, in their last report to Governor Scales, through their chairman, Dr. E. Burke Haywood (almost continuously a member of the Board since 1866), expressed themselves in the following language:

> "The asylum for the care and treatment of the insane has been in operation more than thirty-two years. In our opinion it is now, in all respects, in better condition than it ever was, the percentage of recoveries being larger and that of deaths smaller. It is now ventilated and heated by the best apparatus. The water-works have stood the test of floods and time, and given entire satisfaction. The sewerage is extensive and complete and works admirably," etc., etc.

CHARGES AND CONSPIRACIES.

The opportunity has been found to arraign me for trial upon charges that can only be characterized as both absurd and infamous. Notwithstanding all the history referred to in the preceding pages, well known to those officially connected with the institution as Directors, resident officers and employees, the trouble and trial, which in almost every case attends a protracted service as superintendent of an asylum like this, has come in its turn to me. As the culmination of the prejudices, disappointments and hatreds resulting from the friction incident to necessary discipline of officers and employees, and from the discharge of those who have proven their unfitness for position,

I have been subject to the humiliation of being called upon to answer charges which carry on their face evidences of untruth and vindictiveness. These accusations are trumped up and purport to be based on transactions long past, for the most part four or five years ago, and are the allegations of persons who were conscious of their own shortcomings, and who feared the results of their conduct, which the cloak of charity, at the utmost, could not much longer conceal. I have long suspected that a conspiracy against me existed in the institution, fostered and encouraged by the Second Assistant Physician and Steward. Their reasons seem inexplicable, unless the origin of their course was the fear of the exposure of unjustifiable conduct on their part.

THE CHIEF INSTRUMENT OF THE CONSPIRACY.

Dr. Sion H. Rogers, the main instrument of this conspiracy, and the brain that directed it in its incipiency, came to me when yet a boy and asked to read medicine with me. I took him into the bosom of my family and gave him my utmost confidence.

My instruction and assistance and the use of my library were given to him cheerfully and without charge. After his graduation I informed him that I should use whatever influence lay in my power to secure his appointment as Second Assistant Physician in the institution, and it was upon my nomination that he was elected.

He was taken into my office upon pleasant and confidential relations, and was recommended for re-election. So far all was well, and there was no discernible cause for a rupture of pleasant official relations. On the contrary, I had given a hundred proofs of sincere interest in and desire for the welfare of a young man who had become so closely connected with my life-work under such pleasant circumstances. But occasional lapses from duty on his part, by undesirable and undue attentions to the female attendants, to the breaking down of discipline and the occurrence of scandal in the institution, imperatively demanded interference on my part, and I warned him against too much attention to attendants.

My advice was not taken. His visits within and without the institution and rides and protracted interviews with them continued, notwithstanding the advice and warning of the matron as well as myself.

HIS UNDUE INTIMACY AND INSUBORDINATE CONDUCT.

Afterward a similar set of circumstances connected his name with that of another attendant, whom he met at a dressmaker's in the town of Raleigh, from time to time, and asked for under a feigned name, while still she was an employee at the institution; whom he visited with a telegram at a late hour, on the night before her departure from the Asylum; and with whom he has continued correspondence since her discharge from a position that she was considered disqualified to fill.

Constant accounts of similar conduct came to my knowledge, as well as repeated and continual reports of his comments to the attendants upon the discipline of the institution, directed against the Superintendent and the vigilant care of the matron.

Such a spirit of insubordination and inattention to duty was aroused that it became necessary, as rapidly as their places could be supplied, to discharge some and to request others to resign who were implicated in this neglect and insubordinate spirit. It is hardly necessary to point out that unquestioning obedience to duty is the only safeguard of an institution like this.

PERSISTS IN HIS INSUBORDINATION AND CONTINUES HIS INTRIGUES.

After these attendants resigned or were discharged his attentions to another attendant were of such a character as to excite comment in the institution, and he complained that he had discovered that his interviews with her were watched by other attendants. He visited her after her departure, corresponded with her and endeavored to secure her a position in another asylum.

MY SIN OF HESITATION AND FAULT OF LENIENCY.

I hoped against hope, and made every effort to check and to restrain a course which would lead inevitably to his ruin. It has been the rule of the Asylum ever since I entered its doors that no officer or employee, from the Superintendent down, should enter the room of a female patient without the presence of an attendant also.

This salutary rule, for mutual protection, I have always practiced myself and rigidly enforced as far as I was able. Obliged to withdraw my confidence, once so freely bestowed, I trusted that with a strict curtailment of his privileges, and unceasing vigilance, the errors attributable possibly to his youth and want of experience might become things of the past, and be atoned for by his usefulness eventually in the institution. In this I have been guilty of a fault of judgment in suffering charity to go too far, and am bitterly reaping the consequences.

HIS HATRED FOR THOSE WHO WOULD HAVE SAVED HIM.

He contracted an inveterate hatred to the matron, and infused it into the Steward, whom he seemed to dominate, and over whom his control was apparently unlimited.

I have never been able to find a cause for this hatred except her interest in and oversight of those of the female attendants whom she warned against the excess of attentions that led to scandal in the institution. Doubtless the circumstances alluded to have been occasionally aggravated by the effect upon him of intoxicants.

Upon his joining the staff of the Asylum I advised him to avoid intoxicating liquors, but I regret to say that he has been repeatedly seen under their influence in the city of Raleigh, and has been publicly arrested and taken to the guard-house at the request of a saloon-keeper.

THE CAREER OF AN INGRATE.

This is the career of a young man who once seemed to me to present the promise of a useful and honored physician, and a blessing to the circle in which he moved, but whom it was my imperative duty to check and restrain upon his entrance on a career that promised only disaster for himself and others, and who, in his turn, burns with the intense malignity born of ingratitude.

THE ROLE PLAYED BY THE STEWARD.

Years ago Mr. John W. Thompson was elected Steward. I took him into my confidence and re-nominated him again and again for the office; and he was treated with conspicuous kindness and regard. Upon my motion a Steward's residence was built for the better accommodation of himself and family, in the design of which his wishes were consulted, and in its furniture, so far as economy would allow.

The conveyances of the institution for himself and family were never refused when practicable to accommodate him. Leaves of absence were cheerfully granted, and his duties frequently performed by the Superintendent during such leaves given for his health or pleasure. To increase his efficiency as Steward, and benefit his health, which showed some impairment, he was sent, at my suggestion, to visit various asylums in Alabama, Mississippi, Georgia, etc. Nothing that I could properly do was left undone to promote his welfare. But Mr. Thompson seemed to forget all these services and more—that tie of gratitude that ought to follow my professional services in his family, at a time of extreme anxiety, and most sacred to every honorable and loving husband. In the course of a severe and protracted illness Dr. Rogers was his attending physician, and seemed to obtain complete control of him. After being told of Dr. Rogers' misconduct in the institution a change seemed to pass over him. When informed of Dr. Rogers' misconduct in breaking up the discipline of the institution, and encouraging disrespect toward the matron and Superintendent from the attendants, to my surprise he defended Dr. Rogers.

He further said that he thought that the matron had treated him (the Steward) with disrespect, and by my consent: first, in regard to the care of the calves, and second, in regard to the sending of fruit to his family. It ought to be stated here that during Mr. Thompson's illness the calves, from neglect, had become very poor, and seemed about to die. The matron proposed to nurse, feed and improve them, with the help of the patients, and I consented. They all lived but one; that was too far gone to recover. They had all died the year previous in the same way.

The complaint of the fruit supply was a matter of ordinary care for the patients as our first obligation. The gardener, who is under the direction of the Steward, had been in the habit of sending fruit, such as melons, berries, etc., every day to the families of the Superintendent, Steward and Engineer, and only about twice a week to patients. I directed that he should send all those things to the kitchen, to the care of the housekeeper, who is under the immediate direction of the matron, and that the housekeeper should send to the families of the officers only when such things were also sent to the wards to the patients.

THEY CONSPIRE AGAINST THE MATRON.

Sometime after that, on being asked if Dr. Rogers had not proposed to him to conspire to have the matron turned out of office, he replied that it was no conspiracy, but that Dr. Rogers proposed to him that they should unite to have her turned out of office, and that he had consented. Upon being asked what the matron had done to offend him and Dr. Rogers, he said that he did not think that she was friendly to him, but gave no instance except in regard to the calves and the fruit hereinbefore named, and called it interfering with his business.

INSUBORDINATION OF THE STEWARD.

When fully estranged by the influence of a disappointed and remorseless enemy, evidences of insubordination manifested themselves among those under his immediate control. He approached members of the General Assembly, as he acknowledged to me, with a view of having the organic law changed, to deprive the Superintendent of the nomination of Steward in order to secure his own continued re-election. He invited the tongue of slander to pour into his ear every infamous story his co-conspiraters could conjure, if their testimony is to be believed.

After I had overlooked all this and agreed to his re-election as Steward, upon the suggestion of a prominent member of the Board, he accepted this evidence of forbearance without a change of conduct and with renewed efforts for my destruction.

During my absence he had a personal difficulty with my son, and soon wrote the chairman of the executive committee, which led to the late investigation.

MY ALLEGED INDEBTEDNESS.

In regard to the charge of indebtedness to the Asylum, it is, in any view of the case, simply the remainder of an unpaid debt, which I am ready to settle at any time.

It is altogether based upon whatever action the Board shall take in reference to the refunding of a voluntary discount made upon my salary to avoid, in part, a threatened difficulty in the financial management of the Asylum, on account of the reduction of the appropriation, which trouble never actually occurred.

If the Board shall adjudicate this in my favor, there is no indebtedness, except to myself. If the contrary, I stand ready to obey their wishes, and settle the debt.

THE TURKEY INCIDENT.

It is complained that some turkeys have been given away belonging to the institution. The truth is that some turkeys were purchased by the matron, with her own personal funds, and she raised the young by her own labor, and as an occasional diversion from her exacting and confining labors in-doors. Nearly all these were given to the institution, and used at the meetings of the Board and for the patients. The complete details of this matter are fully exhibited in the statement of the house-keeper appended hereto:

STATEMENT OF W. C. FLETCHER, HOUSEKEEPER.

"I have been housekeeper at the Insane Asylum since 1877, and I have sent to Dr. Grissom's table some pies once a week, cakes occasionally, and now and then, when company was here, some extra things and desserts. This does not include things raised at the institution, to which I have understood Dr. Grissom has a right. Of the turkeys raised here, previous to 1888, Dr. Grissom sent away about six a year.

"In 1888 there were seventy-five turkeys raised here, and Dr. Grissom sent away about twelve, and used twelve at his table. I have often known of Dr. Grissom's entertaining at his own expense visitors of the institution, as those who came to see their relatives who were inmates of the institution. I have also known of Dr. Grissom's entertaining at his own expense many who were in the employ of the institution, as the architect, on more than one occasion, and perhaps as much as two months at one time; the master-builder, on more than two occasions, and for as much perhaps as four months at a time; the florist and others, more than two or three times, and sometimes extendedly. The amount of entertaining of institution guests and those in its employ would repay at least three times the amount sent to Dr. Grissom's table; by this I mean that the amount drawn by Dr. Grissom from the institution would not exceed one-third the amount, I think, that he must have expended in entertaining those above referred to. Moreover, I will state that all the scraps from Dr. Grissom's table have been fed to the hogs and chickens of the institution, and would have more than fed all the turkeys and other fowls used by him. On one occasion, when a present of fresh lamb was sent to Dr. Grissom, he gave it to the institution, amounting to about fifty pounds.

"August 8, 1889. [Signed] "W. C. FLETCHER."

Witness: W. R. CRAWFORD, JR.

"I also give it as my opinion that everything drawn by Dr. Grissom from the institution that came through my department, including that to which he was regularly entitled according to a resolution of the Board of Directors, as well as those articles mentioned in the above certificate, would not equal in value the amount of expense he must have incurred in entertaining visitors to the institution to see their relations, and persons employed in the service of the institution, such as architect, master-builder, etc.

"August 8, 1889. [Signed] "W. C. FLETCHER."

Witness: W. R. CRAWFORD, JR.

MY GIVING AWAY OF SPIRITS.

As to the charge of giving away of spirits, it has reference to the ordinary dispensing of hospitality. On the other hand, I have sometimes supplied to sick patients a better article than was on hand in the institution, and which I have personally bought from the drug store, taking pleasure in furnishing it when I thought their condition demanded its use. Besides, I have also turned over to the institution, absolutely without charge, many medicines and mineral waters sent to me as a personal compliment from various parts of the United States. These were forwarded to me, not as Superintendent of the Asylum, but on account of my connection with a drug store, whose patronage they were soliciting.

THE CHARGE OF CRUELTY.

It is hard to conceive upon what foundation, real or imaginary, the charge of cruelty to the patients can have been based. If it be the death of a patient from heart disease, as I suppose, who had been occasionally placed in restraint to prevent violence to herself and others, in one of her otherwise uncontrollable outbreaks, it is proper to say that the matron and attendants saw her upon the removal of the restraint, and she was as well as at any time, according to all appearances.

The occasional use of restraining apparatus is, by conservative physicians, regarded as just as efficient and salutary as the strong arm of friendship would be to hold back the suicide from the knife, or the water, in his mad effort at self-destruction. To connect it, however remotely, with so ordinary a termination as heart trouble would be ridiculous, if it were not so inhuman a suggestion.

MECHANICAL RESTRAINTS.

This is not the place to discuss the necessity of some method of restraint upon the actions of the insane, so often uncontrollable on their own part, and involving the greatest peril to themselves or others. The subject has been discussed by me in publications hitherto and in the meetings of the American Association of Superintendents of the Insane, with the almost unanimous approval of that body of the views presented. Those who are fully informed on this subject know that the insane were once managed by methods which to us of the present day are revolting and cruel. The benign spirit of modern charity and enlightened science swept away the evil practices of less enlightened days, but extremists in the direction of non-restraint went so far in leaving the insane man to his own devices that the recurrence of suicides and homicides, to say nothing of the obstacles to restoration, soon corrected the effects of the over-enthusiastic in this direction. To-day, both in Europe and America, restraint, either by chemical, manual or mechanical means, is a necessary instrument in the care and cure of a greater or less number of patients in all asylums. It has the testimony in its favor of the most humane and enlightened physicians of the insane in the world. Nor is its approval obsolete and antiquated, as those who accept the theories of writers who know nothing practically of asylum management would pretend to say. The able address of the President of the American Association of Superintendents, only four years ago (Dr. Callender, of Tennessee), reiterates its value, and letters from thirty odd superintendents of the following asylums of the highest character in this country, approving the use of restraint in appropriate cases, have been received by me in the course of this investigation, and were offered in evidence:

Dr. Randolph Barksdale, Superintendent Central Lunatic Asylum, Petersburg, Va.; Dr. G. Alder Blumer, Superintendent State Lunatic Asylum, Utica, N. Y.; Dr. R. M. Bucke, Superintendent Asylum for the Insane, London, Ontario; Dr. H. A. Buttolph, ex-Superintendent; Dr. Michael Campbell, Superintendent Hospital for the Insane, Knoxville, Tenn.; Dr. F. H. Clarke, Superintendent Eastern Kentucky Lunatic Asylum, Lexington, Ky.; Dr. Daniel Clark, Superintendent Asylum for the Insane, Toronto; Dr. Edward Cowles, Superintendent McLean Asylum, Somerville, Mass.; Dr. Theo. W. Fisher, Superintendent Boston Lunatic Hospital, Boston, Mass.; Dr. W. W. Godding, Superintendent Government Hospital for the Insane, Washington, D. C.; Dr. P. E. Griffin, Superintendent South Carolina Lunatic Asylum, Columbia, S. C.; Dr.

H. C. Harris, Superintendent State Asylum for the Insane, Morris Plains, N. J.; Dr. G. H. Hill, Superintendent Hospital for the Insane, Independence, Iowa; Dr. H. B. Hill (in the absence of Dr. Bigelow T. Sanborn), Superintendent Maine Insane Hospital, Augusta, Me.; Dr. Henry M. Hurd, Superintendent Eastern Michigan Asylum, Pontiac, Michigan; Dr. A. E. MacDonald, General Superintendent New York City Asylums for the Insane, New York, N. Y.; Dr. Carlos F. MacDonald, Superintendent State Asylum for Insane Criminals, Auburn, N. Y.; Dr. Andrew McFarland, Superintendent Oak Lawn Retreat for the Insane, Jacksonville, Ill.; Dr. C. A. Miller, Superintendent Longview Asylum, Carthage, Ohio; Dr. T. J. Mitchell, Superintendent Mississippi State Lunatic Asylum, Jackson, Miss.; Dr. J. D. Moncure, Superintendent Eastern Lunatic Asylum, Williamsburg, Va.; Dr. James D. Munson, Superintendent Northern Michigan Asylum, Traverse City, Michigan; Dr. C. H. Nichols, Superintendent Bloomingdale Asylum, New York, N. Y.; Dr. Geo. C. Palmer, Superintendent Michigan Asylum for the Insane, Kalamazoo, Michigan; Dr. C. A. Rice, Superintendent East Mississippi Insane Asylum, Meridian, Miss.; Dr. A. B. Richardson, Superintendent Athens Asylum for the Insane, Athens, Ohio; Dr. Bigelow T. Sanborn, Superintendent Maine Insane Hospital, Augusta, Maine; Dr. C. W. Stevens, Superintendent Lunatic Asylum, St. Louis, Mo.; Dr. H. A. Tobey, Superintendent Toledo Asylum for the Insane, Toledo, Ohio; Dr. John W. Ward, Superintendent New Jersey State Lunatic Asylum, Trenton, New Jersey.

Mechanical restraint was used in this Asylum before my connection with it, and has been applied by its physicians during my incumbency, whenever necessity required it. The North Carolina Insane Asylum, I am thankful to say, has an almost unprecedented record in its freedom from suicides or homicides during my career as Superintendent for twenty-one years. As was well said by Hon. Thos. J. Jarvis, of my counsel, it will be a sad day for the unfortunate insane and their friends in North

Carolina when the beneficent effect of restraint upon those who cannot control their own action is lost, and the dire results of yielding to theorists shall be felt too late. Its use here is much less than formerly, and never except for the good of the patient.

OF CRIMINAL INTIMACY.

The infamous charge of criminal intimacy is brought against one who has been twenty-one years Superintendent of this institution, and now, at the age of more than fifty-eight years, is confronted with an accusation so vile as to be beyond the pale of recognition. This is the first time in my life that any charge of improper conduct of this character has ever been made, even by my bitterest enemies.

The conspirators seem to have forgotten in this desperate and almost demented assault upon me that I have always obeyed implicitly the rule I have prescribed for others—never to enter a female patient's room alone, or to see a female patient alone, under any circumstances. Kind Providence seemed to have thus provided a shelter from the impotent shafts of malice from a score of years ago to the present hour.

* * * * "No, 'tis slander;
Whose edge is sharper than the sword; whose tongue
Out-venoms all the worms of Nile; whose breath
Rides on the posting winds, and doth belie
All corners of the world; kings, queens and states,
Maids, matrons, nay, the secrets of the grave,
Viperous slander enters."

DEFAMING AN INSANE WOMAN.

The character of this prosecution sufficiently manifested itself by its hyena-like conduct in going into the living tomb of a mentally dead woman and attempting ruthlessly to blast her reputation in a desperate effort to convict me of this charge. Of the one hundred and fifty lady attendants of this institution during my residence in it, they selected this poor unfortunate as the one with whom I was alleged to have been seen in criminal intercourse. She is dead to the world. She could neither speak in her defence nor confront her accusers. I had treated her for a disease peculiar to women in the matron's room, and known to the matron.

SACRED RELATIONS OF PHYSICIAN AND PATIENT.

It suited their purpose to torture the confidential relations and private examinations of the physician into illicit intercourse. What would the world be to-day if at every sick chamber of the land the eye of villainous menials should be glued to the key-hole of the room of the suffering; if the tongue of slander whispered its suspicions against every household into which the physician should enter? Have we fallen upon times wherein nothing is sacred and no one honorable? Are the women of the land who must undergo examination and treatment for disease to lose their character and reputation for chastity? Should the physician who goes out to relieve the suffering and distress of women march from the chamber of the invalid to the prison dock of crime or the pillory of infamy? God forbid that men overtaken in crime themselves should be able to compel a public sentiment so vicious in itself and repugnant to the dictates of humanity!

OF CRUELTY TO PATIENTS.

But they accuse me of cruelty to patients. For twenty-one years I have been Superintendent. During that time the Boards have never had less than two regular meetings, and often as many as three or four special ones per year, amounting in the aggregate to not less than sixty or seventy; and on every such occasion the Board, or an intelligent committee of the Board, have visited the wards at will. Besides these there have been numerous official visits on the part of individual members of the Boards or of the Executive Committees. And during this long period and under these varying circumstances how does it happen that not a single instance of abuse or mistreatment of patients has ever been seen or complained of till now? Have the Boards of Directors for twenty years, composed as they have been, of intelligent, high-toned and philanthropic gentlemen, intrusted with responsible and important duties, been unable to discover or discern the least evidence of the high offences charged by these conspirators? How is it that these things have never been noticed by any other resident officers of the institution?

Many of the official visits were made at times by former members of the Board not altogether friendly to the Superintendent for political reasons, and under circumstances that gave them access to the private ear of every employee and patient in the institution. But no such suspicion ever crossed their minds. There have been treated here during my administration over 1,400 patients, representing families in every county in North Carolina, and strange to say, if these abuses existed, not one word of complaint reached official ears.

EXAMINATIONS BY LEGISLATIVE COMMITTEES.

During my entire incumbency the whole management and conduct of the Insane Asylum has been the subject of an inquisition as searching as any system of investigation ever designed. Each Legislature constituted a standing committee of both Houses on the Asylum of gentlemen of all political parties and of varied elements.

The examinations and investigations of these legislative committees were always thorough, and the inspection of the Asylum complete. They had access to and saw or had an opportunity of seeing every officer, employee and patient in the institution.

How is it that in all these years the inquisitorial committee of the Legislature found none of these things alleged to have existed so long by the conspirators? As a result of all these searching examinations favorable reports were made on all occasions.

NOT A SINGLE PATIENT TO ACCUSE ME.

During the twenty-one years past there have been under my charge 1,400 patients, representing families in every county in

North Carolina, twenty-five per cent. of whom have been discharged cured. Not one of these did the prosecutors introduce upon the witness stand to establish their charges of cruelty against me.

During the same period there have been more than 150 female attendants, yet from that great number of reputable working women only one, and she discharged for cause, could they find to accuse me; and she, it was proven by a minister of the Gospel, was speaking in the highest and most complimentary terms of me the day before her discharge. These charges of mistreatment and cruelty to patients embrace allegations of circumstances pretended to have occurred five or six years ago. During all this period, notwithstanding many meetings of the Board and several sessions of the General Assembly, no charges, no intimations of any such occurrences were made by these officers. On the contrary, they have been the recipients of many kindnesses and favors, in daily personal and official intercourse with me, and have gladly received nomination annually at my hands, to the very positions which placed them under the superintendency of one whom they now accuse of extreme cruelty and gross mistreatment of the patients for whom in a measure they were morally responsible. By their own statement, therefore, they are grossly corrupt and untrustworthy, or else their charges are fabrications dexterously annexed to occasional duties which the salutary restraint of an asylum requires, to preserve the lives of patients and promote their welfare.

AFFECTION OF PATIENTS FOR THE SUPERINTENDENT—A COMMENTARY UPON THE CHARGE OF CRUELTY.

Let any intelligent enemy of mine, the bitterest and most vindictive, pass through these wards, and he will witness a devotion to me on the part of these patients not surpassed in any institution of the United States. The only feeling of hostility that has ever manifested itself here, has been on the part of subordinate officials and employees, who were disciplined, discharged, or in fear of losing their places for misconduct. There have been throughout my administration several hundred attendants and employees, of both colors and sexes, in constant attendance upon the patients, both night and day, and, strange to say, it remains for this occasion and these suspicious surroundings for such accusations to be made. Can any intelligent, virtuous man for one moment believe them to be true?

But I am accused of immorality. For twenty years I have been the employee of these Boards of Directors, under every administration and both parties, and not one word of suspicion has ever been uttered by any responsible party reflecting upon my moral conduct. For twenty years there have been employed in the institution female attendants from various sections of the State, representing many varieties of character and temperament, and to the number of more than one hundred and fifty, many of whom have gone into active society, some of whom have been discharged, and others are still here; and it remains until now, under the present surroundings, for any charge of this sort to be made. For almost a quarter of a century have I gone in and out before this community, and, owing to the position I occupy, to a certain extent "the observed of all observers," and under the watchful eye of both friend and foe, and now, at the advanced age of nearly sixty years, after this long career of public service, it remains for this occasion and under these surroundings and by these parties, to discover that my conduct has been immoral. Such a conclusion stultifies the observation and discrimination of a long line of Directors, a long list of employees, and of an entire public.

STATEMENT OF J. A. TUCKER, CHIEF ATTENDANT.

To throw farther light upon the methods of the conspirators, and especially of Dr. Rogers, the following statement of J. A. Tucker, chief male attendant at the Asylum, is presented:

"AUGUST 10th, 1889.

"*Dr. Eugene Grissom:*

"SIR:—* * * * * * * * * * *

As you know, Doctor, I had to report to and be with your enemies a good portion of the time. I was asked by them, or one of them at least, time and again, about this affair. I would always answer that you had been as kind and treated me as well as I wished to be by any one, and that I knew nothing derogatory of you in any respect. I was with Dr. Rogers in his daily visits through the wards, when he would, when talking to attendants whom he knew to be hostile towards you, cast insinuations upon me for keeping silent and not taking any part in this affair. I took no notice of them whatever.

After awhile he asked me to go over to Mr. Whitaker's office and state to him what I knew about the institution (I say he asked me, but Mr. Norwood asked me at his request). I told him that I knew nothing that would be of any advantage to them. This was on Monday, and they wanted me to go that night; I did not go; on Wednesday I went for the purpose of giving in my tax, and while in the court-house was asked by a man, whom I have since learned was Mr. Spier Whitaker, about the Nutt affair, the restraint and your immorality; the answer to which you already know.

Besides having such as this to contend with, I was a portion of the time in a ward with Mr. Norwood, who was anything but friendly toward you, and who tried in various ways to draw some expression or statement from me derogatory of you and to influence me against you. Nay, Doctor, what I want to show you is that, notwithstanding all their combined efforts to prejudice me against you, that my feelings toward you are as good as they are toward any living man, and I respect you both as a superior and a friend—for such you have proven yourself to be, and I feel very grateful for it. * * *

"I remain yours, obediently, J. A. TUCKER."

As a farther commentary on this subject, the following extracts are made from statements by several attendants, made subsequently to the late investigation:

STATEMENTS OF OTHER ATTENDANTS.

Under date of July 31st, 1889, Mr. J. E. Carroll acknowledges having gone to Mr. Spier Whitaker's office, at the request of Mr. J. A. Norwood (who was one of the instruments employed by Dr. Rogers). After stating the inquiries made of him, and replies, he adds:

"I repeat that I have never known of any immorality or mistreatment of patients on the part of Dr. Grissom.

(Signed) "J. E. CARROLL."

August 1st, 1889, Mr. J. H. Williams, another attendant, made a statement in writing, from which the following paragraph is taken:

"I was not examined on either side in the late trial. Dr. Rogers, sometime previous to the trial, asked me if I had seen or known anything wrong about the institution, or something to that effect. I made a reply that showed that I knew nothing of the character that he desired. * * * I have never seen any cruelty or abuse of patients on the part of Dr. Grissom, and have never seen him lay his hands upon any one. I have never known of any immorality on his part, and had never suspicioned such a thing until I heard the charges. (Signed) "J. H. WILLIAMS."

Under date of August 1st, Mr. E. C. Moring states that he has never seen any cruelty to patients, or known of any immorality of any kind on the part of Dr. Grissom.

Mr. G. W. Goodwin (August 3d, 1889) has made a similar statement, closing with the emphatic declaration that

"I have never seen you mistreat any patient nor use cruelty to any patient nor handle any patient roughly, nor do I know of you having taken any liberties with any female attendants or others. I repeat that I have never known of any cruelty or immorality on the part of Dr. Grissom.

"G. W. GOODWIN."

Mr. W. C. Betts, in a statement made August 1st, 1889, writes as do all the others, adding as follows:

"Mr. Norwood was related to Dr. Rogers, and I suppose that had something to do with his unfriendliness. * * * * * * * * *

"I have never seen any cruelty to or mistreatment of, nor rough handling of the patients on the part of Dr. Grissom, nor do I know of any immorality or improper advances to female attendants or others.

"August 3d, 1889. "W. C. BETTS."

These efforts to prejudice the attendants and obtain farther suborned testimony are worthy of the man who was seen on some occasions to examine my private mail, at a late hour of the night.

The statements herewith given are in addition to the evidence in my defence in the official investigation. Additional papers are in my possession, but it does not seem necessary to add anything more.

CHARACTER AND FAITHFUL PUBLIC SERVICE WORTH NOTHING.

If, in view of all these facts, such a prosecution as this, instigated by vengeance, one of the strongest passions of the human mind, and sustained by discharged and disappointed employees, shall accomplish its end, then an honorable life, faithful public service, self-sacrifice to duty, virtuous conduct, and the good opinion of one's fellow-men are all worthless and in vain, when assailed by the breath of scandal, prompted by vindictiveness and malice.

WHAT THESE PROSECUTORS AND CONSPIRATORS KNOW.

These prosecutors know, these discharged employees know, their sympathizers and abettors know, as they know they are living men, that I have never mistreated any patients intentionally and have never used any force toward them except what was necessary for their control. They know that I have been guilty of no immoral conduct in this institution. They know that the late prosecution is unjust and vindictive. And they know that the evidence they have offered and encouraged is untrue, and may God Almighty forgive them the falsehood of their testimony.

A CLUE TO THE SUPPORT OF THE CONSPIRACY.

The proceedings of the Board of Directors of the Insane Asylum furnish a clue to an element of support in this conspiracy, and I beg leave to submit here some matters of record:

"At the annual meeting of the Board of Directors of the Insane Asylum of North Carolina, held at that institution on Wednesday, December 4, 1878, the following were present, to-wit: Dr. E. Burke Haywood, Dr. J. T. Leach, Mr. Julius Lewis, Col. J. G. Burr, Maj. C. Dowd and Col. Jas. S. Amis. Dr. E. Burke Haywood being in the chair, the meeting was called to order and the following business transacted:

"* * * * Col. Burr offered the following resolution:

"'WHEREAS, It is known to the public that a controversy has been going on between Dr. Eugene Grissom, the Superintendent of the Asylum for the Insane of North Carolina, and Dr. W. A. Hammond, of New York City, in which the latter has made charges of a most injurious character, not only as to the professional, but also the personal reputation of Dr. Grissom, and by implication has attempted to convey the impression that the patients of this Asylum under his care have been subjected to cruel treatment; therefore,

"'*Resolved,* That we hereby re-assert our confidence in Dr. Grissom, and that these insinuations in relation to the ill treatment of the patients of this Asylum are untrue in every particular, and that we fully concur in the statement made by the Executive Committee to Dr. Grissom under date of July 19, 1878.

"'*Resolved further,* That as members of the Board of Directors of the Insane Asylum of North Carolina and as citizens watchful of the management of the institution committed to our care, and jealous of the honor of the State, we feel proud of the manner in which Dr. Grissom has conducted this controversy, sustained as he is by some of the ablest medical journals of the country and most distinguished members of his profession, reflecting credit alike upon himself and the State of North Carolina.' Carried unanimously."

STATEMENT OF THE EXECUTIVE COMMITTEE.

The following is the statement of the Executive Committee referred to in the proceedings:

"*Dr. Eugene Grissom, Superintendent of the Insane Asylum of North Carolina:*

DEAR SIR:—Yours of this date to hand, in which you call our attention to the fact that in a recently published 'Open Letter' addressed to you by Dr. Hammond, of New York, he, by implication, charges you with cruelty to the patients in our Asylum. As the local members of the Executive Committee of the Board of Directors we have at all times free access to the Asylum, and frequently visit and are brought in contact with the patients, attendants and officers and all others connected with the institution, and we have never heard from any one even an intimation of unkindness, much less cruelty, on your part or any other officer's, but, on the contrary, we have every reason to believe that in your intercourse with and treatment of the unfortunate ones under your care you are uniformly kind and considerate, doing everything in your power for their relief and comfort. Yours truly, etc.,

"(Signed) A. M. MCPHEETERS,
JULIUS LEWIS,
Executive Committee."

"RALEIGH, July 19, 1878.

THE ALLY OF THE PROSECUTION.

There is little room to doubt that one of the encouragements to this assault upon me relates back to the Hammond controversy. He had himself preferred these charges of cruelty and of personal misconduct through the medium of his "Open Letter," and he would, of course, welcome and reward the co-operation of any one who would undertake to establish what he vainly sought through his publication of a dozen years ago. Hence, while the conspiracy against me has been uncovered here at home, I must maintain that its encouragement may have been from a distant enemy with a mortal grievance against me.

THE COUNSEL FOR THE PROSECUTION ACKNOWLEDGED THE RECEPTION OF LARGE FEES.

It is well known that Dr. Rogers and Mr. Thompson were not pecuniarily able to pay, without aid, large fees to their counsel. But in addition to this large sums for necessary expenses were disbursed in behalf of the prosecution. Who supplied the money? The counsel-in-chief quoted Dr. Hammond. His argument gave evidence of the source of its inspiration. His authorities were Hammond's books, and his criticisms upon the use of restraint in the care of the insane were the natural product of Hammond's theories and suggestions.

A RUINED WOMAN TO GIVE MANUFACTURED EVIDENCE ON DR. ROGERS' INSTRUCTIONS.

It is necessary, in order to exhibit the method of manufacturing evidence and the infamous means employed in this conspiracy for my ruin, to refer to circumstances of personal history bearing upon the movements of Dr. Sion H. Rogers and one of his victims. As I judged that the usefulness of an attendant in the institution was at an end, she was required to resign, in July, 1888. Correspondence between Dr. Rogers and herself was maintained, and he visited her at her home, in February last, and assisted her to secure a position in the Central Lunatic Asylum, at Lakeland, Ky. But there came, speedily, a time when public employment was no longer practicable. The victim was overcome with a shame that she could not conceal in public, and she must need seek seclusion. Poor, trusting woman, she turned to the author of her ruin for help, comfort and protection. She might as well have appealed to an insensible rock for the sympathy of true manhood. Throughout his response there is not a sentiment dissociated from the schemes of his own ambition and gratification of his own passions.

THE BOLD, CALCULATING LETTER OF A LIBERTINE AND CRIMINAL.

(*Literal Copy.*)

"North Carolina Insane Asylum,
"Raleigh, N. C., June 12, 1889.

"Dear May:—I received your letter on Monday. I was particularly glad to hear from you, as you were so distressed when you wrote before, and I felt anxious about you. I fear I cannot write you such a letter as I would like to-night, but must write you some any way. It is useless for me to go over what would have been best, etc. The thing now is for us to make the best we can of things as they are. As I understand your letter, the plan of your coming here is now to be carried out and soon. I will try to get a place as soon as possible—when I have done so I will let you know—the thing then will be for you to arrange to come—several things are necessary. In the meantime write to your people in a manner to show that you don't feel satisfied there even to the extent of saying if you can find another place you think you would like you would go to it. Let Mary DeVane, and any people you are in the habit of talking to, know that your mother talks of wanting you to come home, so that they won't be too much surprised when you tell them that you are going. I think that would probably be a good plan (*i. e.*) to let them think there you have gone home.

"When the time comes to start you can tell them you will pass through M & H. P., but instead of the real time put it a day or two later, and then after you have gotten here you can write to them and tell them of your mistake. I know no other way to do. Of course, May, I feel worried about this as much as you do—but, as I have told you, I want to do all I can for you—and I shall. As is always the case, everything comes at once. I have told you of my money troubles, and now matters here have about come to a head, and the final contest with this old scoundrel here is about to come, and in a short time either he or I must step out. The affairs here come before the Board in a short time. If I can prove enough of his villainy, he must go. If not, then I must. I will see now who will stand by me. I expect you to do so for one —and before I finish this letter I will suggest to you what you can do to help me most now, all things considered. Your condition precludes your doing all you otherwise might—yet you may be of considerable service.

"You can see that this makes it all the more necessary for no one to find out anything about your condition, etc. Let me know if it will be necessary for me to send you any money to get here, and if so, how much. Of course it would make it more troublesome to conceal if I send you money, as some one might find it out, and that might excite suspicion—a money order, or anything of that kind, it would not do for me to send at all—tho' I might do as I did when you went out, just enclose it in a letter—that is risky. It is all hard on us and bad for us, May, but in spite of all that it has some brightness any way. You will be glad to see me and I to see you—there will be times when we will forget all but pleasure we have together, and we will be happy then some even if we are anxious and uneasy.

"You will pet me and I you, and we will have some good times anyway—no matter what comes. We must hope for the best, and if we pull through all right, and no one ever finds it out, it won't make any difference, and we will have had some pleasure as well as trouble and pain. In regard to this rascal here—I want you to write me a letter now, just like you were writing it at home soon after you left here. Date it High Point, Aug. 20, '88 (that was soon after you left here). Say in your own way that since you have been home you have wanted to write to me and tell me some things that you were ashamed to tell me when you were here, because you were afraid I would blame you for having stayed here after such things occurred, but that you feel like some one ought to know how mean Dr. Grissom is; that you have told me some of his meanness the way he did Hattie and some things he did to you, but not half of them—then go on and tell me the various things he did, about his kissing you in the office when you went there to report to him, trying to get you in his lap after sending you up to the Matron's room like he wanted to see you on business, and many or all such things he did to you be plain, May, and do not keep back any of it. It may be no one but me will ever see the letter or know anything of it. It may be I would have to use it to help fix him—whichever it is I must have all these things I can get, for when the fight comes it will be to the death for him or for me—and if I have a Friend he or she must help me in this; then if you have ever seen him strike or beat or kick or choke or otherwise mistreat a patient, tell me about that and the patient's name—those things may be of value to me—then wind up by saying you hope I will not think less of you for having not told these things, for I knew your helpless condition, and how afraid of him you were, and every time anything of the sort occurred you tried to keep him from it and hoped it would be the last time; then say you were actually afraid to go to the office for anything, and afraid if he came in a ward you were in charge of; then say that you were not the only one he treated that way, and that no one knows what we poor girls had to go through with down there, that you hope some day he will meet his just reward—and that you hope I will not blame you for not having left before and told why you left etc.

"Begin your letter simply—Dr. Rogers—and end respectfully yours. I have written this sketch of the letter I want you to write me so you can see what I do want.

"Of course, if you have never seen him strike or choke or abuse a patient you just say nothing about that, but I know you have seen him do so. You understand I want the letter such a one as I could show the Board if it became necessary, and of course you write it just as if you had done it without my asking you any questions. Tell me all you know in these bad things his abuse of patients and his improper advances or liberties with you, etc. Write this as soon as you can and enclose it in your letter to me—send all your letters like you did your last—to W. H. Weaver, Capitol Club. Good night. Be cheerful and bright as you can.

"Let us hope for the best and we may come out all right and may give this old scoundrel what he deserves. Write soon, and believe me always,

"Yours sincerely,

"(Signed) S. H. Rogers."

THE AUTHENTICITY OF THE LETTER.

This letter, proven by Mr. John W. Thompson on the witness stand to be in the handwriting of and signature of Dr. Sion H. Rogers, was picked up in or near the night attendant's room at the Central Lunatic Asylum, Lakeland, Kentucky, by one of the supervisors and forwarded to Raleigh. There is no doubt about its authenticity. It came to me as a voluntary contribution to the strength of my defence.

It was not such a letter as a betrayed woman would cherish or take pains to preserve. Its very hollow-heartedness, selfish calculation, false pretence and lascivious revelling in the very hour of heavy travail, were enough to have caused the unfortunate woman to cast it away in disgust. Mark the final injunction of this unsavory letter! "Send to W. H. Weaver, Capitol Club." W. H. Weaver is a colored servant in the employment of the club. What could have been the motive that inspired the direction in this letter to "Dear May" to deceive her invalid mother at High Point and to come to Raleigh or its vicinity? With whom was she to find refuge, and with what object?

THE APPROPRIATE SPHERE OF PUBLIC INDIGNATION.

Public indignation should be swift to visit with its sharpest punishment him who beguiles the affections of young and unprotected women thrown upon the world and compelled to wring from its hard conditions a living for themselves and dependent relatives; and who goes on his way, careless of the ruin he has wrought as the price of the gratification of his momentary caprice or his baser passions.

It is one of the melancholy incidents of the unraveling of this conspiracy that the shafts of the libertine aimed at me have been more fatal to his weaker victims.

THE KEY TO THE WHOLE EVIDENCE OF THE PROSECUTION.

The letter of Dr. Rogers is a key to the whole evidence against me on the charges of immorality and cruelty. It fixes clearly the fact that he was the manufacturer of the evidence to fit the charges he formulated. No one who heard the testimony or read it and the letter together could come to any other conclusion.

It is possible that there are those who may be led by this cunningly devised letter to suppose that the unfortunate woman who was thus instructed by Dr. Rogers really knew something to my discredit which ought to weigh against me, whatever blame may attach to Rogers and others. The device is too transparent to affect many minds, but to fully settle any possible misgiving in any honest mind, the following statement is hereby appended, of the recipient of the letter from Dr. Rogers, given on June 24th, 1889, on the train bound for Knoxville, Tenn., from Louisville, Ky.:

STATEMENT OF MISS MAY ———.

"I entered employ of the Asylum about the last of July, 1886; stayed two years; was in the first, second and fifth wards; was night attendant for awhile; never knew Dr. Grissom to mistreat any of the patients; never knew him to interview a patient in a room alone, and he did not allow others to do so; never knew Dr. Grissom to be guilty of drunkenness; never knew Dr. Grissom to fail to investigate any charges of cruelty to patients.

"Mr. Eugene Grissom, Jr., has treated me fairly and gentlemanly in this interview. Never saw any unnecessary restraint or any that was cruel.

"The above is a correct copy of a conversation between Mr. Eugene Grissom, Jr., and myself, upon train bound for Knoxville, Tenn., June 24th, 1889.

"Witnesses: "MAY ———.

"MARY DEVANE,

"EUGENE GRISSOM, JR.

"June 24th, 1889.

"Miss May ——— adds that she has never seen any improper relations on the part of Dr. Grissom with any female attendants.

"Witnesses: "MAY ———.

"EUGENE GRISSOM, JR.,

"MARY DEVANE."

To this is appended the following statement made since date of above:

"HIGH POINT, N. C., July 13th, 1889.

"*Mr. Eugene Grissom, Jr.:*

"DEAR SIR:—You requested me to make a statement of what I have heard Dr. Rogers say about Dr. Grissom and the matron. I cannot recall much that I have ever heard him say about them. I have heard him say that Dr. Grissom was a rascal, and have heard him call the matron a hell cat.

"Respectfully, "MAY ———."

It is not necessary that I should traverse the evidence of this protracted trial. My counsel have done this fully, as every reader will see from their speeches during the trial. As regards the charges of embezzlement of supplies, they were so trivial and childish that I will not take up time with them further.

THE CHARACTER OF MR. THOMPSON.

Mr. John W. Thompson has enjoyed the reputation of an honest man. I have regarded him the dupe of a superior mind and the simple tool of a designing man. But when the letter of the libertine disclosed to Mr. Thompson, as to all men, the deep-laid plot, why did not he wash his hands of the revealed conspirator, and disavow the conspiracy? Why did he, and how could he still, maintain the relation of friend and co-operator even to the point of resigning in company with him and in letters of the same apparent mental preparation and probable parentage?

Mr. Thompson has chosen to take and keep his stand with Dr. Rogers and with him to sink into the depths of infamy. At the moment of resignation from a position which he saw it to be practically impossible to hold he insulted the entire Board by a communication in which, among other ebullitions of malice and disappointment, he declared his unwillingness to keep the legally authorized system of accounts as approved by them, which he never had a criticism for during the series of years in which he kept and desired to retain his comfortable office.

This conduct, together with his other reflections and those of his partner and friend, Dr. Rogers, the Board, in its self-respect, properly treated by unanimously resolving to return the communications as unworthy of reception, and accepting their proffered resignations instantly, and under such circumstances as to amount to dismissal.

THE CHARACTER OF THE PROSECUTION.

And it is by men like these I am accused. I am charged and arraigned for trial by Dr. Sion H. Rogers and Mr. John W. Thompson. The former, the author of the letter to "Dear May," dared not appear upon the witness stand; the other proved absolutely nothing of his own knowledge, yet, in the face of this, despite the array of testimony in my favor and a verdict of vindication at the hands of the Board, there are public papers and public sentiment in the State pronouncing me guilty of all the charges and of every specification. Denunciation of myself and impeachment of my character have rung from one end of the State to the other, and indignation meetings have been called by the thoughtless and the uninformed to express their excited feelings over imaginary outrages. And all this upon the arraignment of a self-convicted seducer and procurer of false testimony, his victims, tools, and followers. Was snch a spectacle ever before witnessed within the borders of a State so conservative and law-abiding?

HIGH CHARACTER OF BOARDS OF DIRECTORS.

Under all the changes of party, and throughout all the mutations of public sentiment, the Boards of Directors of the Insane Asylum have been constituted of the best material of the State. The character of no Board ever has or ever can be impeached before the people of North Carolina. The present organization is no exception to those which have preceded it.

MY VINDICATION.

E. Burke Haywood, M. D., LL. D., for these many years President of the Board, long among the most distinguished medical men of the State and a distinguished surgeon in the Confederate service, is a gentleman of such Christian worth and exalted personal character that no man can whisper the suspicion of an insinuation against him or impeach his intelligence or discriminating, uncompromising judgment.

Col. James S. Amis, of Granville, for many years before and during the war a leading member of the General Assembly, a member of the Board since 1877, is a leading lawyer of the State, a man of the highest sense of honor and personal probity, a Christian and a philanthropist, against whose name and character there is no whisper, and throughout his long and honored career no man has ever found cause for the slightest allegation prejudicial to the conduct and bearing of a noble gentleman.

Dr. John McCormick, of Harnett, is as honorable a gentleman as the State holds within her borders. He is old in the public service, having repeatedly served Harnett and Cumberland in the Legislature in both branches of the General Assembly, and has served on these Boards through successive years of Executive confidence. Any impeachment of his character, understanding or sense of justice would be outrageous treason against the people of a section of the State noted for standing and worth for two centuries.

Capt. W. S. Harris, of Franklin, is likewise an old public servant and a senior member of this Board. He has represented the counties of Franklin, Nash and Wilson in the Legislature, was a distinguished soldier of the war, and a man in whom his neighbors have the most implicit confidence, and in intellect, worth and personal probity the equal of any man in the State.

Dr. Isaac Jackson, of Columbus, is a native of Chatham, of a family distinguished for its traits of personal honor and of high public character. He is a junior member of the Board.

but is here in obedience to the united voice of the people of his adopted section, and his credentials of character are as high as were ever borne to the State Capital in the public service.

The voice of these gentlemen was pronounced in my vindication.

FOR CONVICTION.

Dr. W. R. Capehart, of Bertie, a citizen of character and standing, is a senior member of the Board, but did not appear at the trial in obedience to the official summons, nor until urged to do so by the counsel for the prosecution, as follows:

Received 10:05 A. M.—Mail—Williamston.

Dated: RALEIGH, N. C., June 27th, 1889.

To Dr. W. R. Capehart,

Avoca, Bertie county, N. C.:

We again appeal to you to come and assume the responsibilities and perform the duties of your trust.

C. M. BUSBEE,
SPIER WHITAKER,

Dr. Capehart voted against me on the charge of immorality, the principal testimony in favor of which he did not hear nor did he have the opportunity to see the demeanor of the witnesses on the stand. On the other charges he sustained me.

Mr. Richard H. Smith, of Halifax, is a man of character. But he is a man of very advanced age, nearly seventy-eight years, into whose ears for some time previous to this investigation the conspirators or their agents had poured rumors of scandal.

Dr. George A. Foote, of Warren, the last member in attendance upon the Board, is understood to have been a candidate for the position of Superintendent of the Asylum for many years. He voted against me on all the charges, as was expected. During the hearing of the evidence for the defense he absented himself, and went home, and paid little or no attention to the arguments of defendant's counsel.

ACQUIESCENCE IN THE PUBLIC WILL.

While I am at all times ready to acquiesce in the will of the people, in regard to the management of their institution, supported by the taxation of their property, yet I do not regard that will as expressed by demonstrations made in so-called indignation meetings in certain parts of the State, in which the action of the Board of Directors has been criticised in a manner scarcely respectful to law itself. Nor do I regard these meetings as being a fair representation of either the virtue or intelligence of their respective communities, and especially is this the case of those held in Raleigh and Wake county.

UNAUTHORIZED PUBLICATION.

It is not improper that I should mention the fact that I have received during the progress and since the trial, letters of sympathy and congratulation from almost every section of the State. Some of these names I collected in the form of a printed letter, directed to the patrons and friends of the institution to counteract some of the evil influences of the slanders, falsehoods and detractions against the management of the institution. This was a private letter put in printed form for convenience. One of these letters was obtained from some source by one Josephus Daniels and published in his newspaper. It is to be hoped that he is the only editor capable of committing such an impropriety. The editor of another paper in Raleigh, equally hostile to me, sought permission to publish this letter, but upon being refused abstained until seeing it in the paper above referred to.

POSTSCRIPT.

The appointment of two members of the Board of Directors of the Asylum out of the number who approved my official course and vindicated my character in the recent investigation of the affairs of the institution by the Governor of the State to positions on the Board of Public Charities, coupled with the high appreciation justly expressed of Dr. E. Burke Haywood's official career and his long continued service in the cause of charity, would seem to my friends and the public to set the seal of Executive approval to their course in acquitting me of the charges presented by the late conspiracy of subordinate officers in this institution.

But when it is perceived that these gentlemen and other members of the Board have been informed that under the technicalities of law they cannot serve as Directors of the Asylum and have no right farther to perform the duties of the same on the ground of holding such positions as Physician of the Deaf and Dumb, County Superintendent of Health and the like, coupled with the nomination to the vacancies made in this manner, of gentlemen well known to be hostile to me, such as Capt. Octavius Coke, the leader of a partisan movement in the Legislature of 1877, to deprive me of the position of Superintendent, because of my political affiliations, before assuming the control of this sacred charity, and of Thomas B. Womack, who does not scruple to accept place as a Director of this Asylum after having denounced me in a public meeting, and published over his own signature a scheme for my removal, the true intent and the political bearing of such appointments are revealed.

While appearing to compliment my friends, and indirectly, at least, to approve their official conduct by the tender of what might be regarded as promotion, the intent is, through some possible means, to reverse their action, and attain the ends of what has been converted into a semi-political persecution.

I am frank to say that the clamors of the ignorant and misled, under the tutelage of interested or of deeply prejudiced parties, would never have affected my resolution to retain my present position, under the control of any fair-minded Board, and especially of those gentlemen who have conducted its affairs for years with the most intimate knowledge of its history, and who honor me with their confidence and support to the present hour, as always heretofore.

But when a sufficient number of these faithful public servants have been informed that they are to be forced out of position from having inadvertently held some other place, and are refused the right to remain where they are because their appointment or election to other office has been subsequent to their appointment upon the Board of Directors of the Asylum, it becomes my duty and pleasure to retire with them, and not remain to subject myself to a hostile Board, appointed to attain personal and political ends, and to render the successful administration of the Asylum impossible by the embarrassment of my management, which it would be in their power to effect.

It is therefore my purpose to resign the superintendency of this institution.

It remains to be seen whether the same technicality of law will receive the attention of the Executive in the cases of the State officers, judges, legislative and executive officials of every description, embracing a large number of the most eminent officials of the State government, who hold such positions as directors of State institutions, trustees of the State University, and of the State Agricultural and Mechanical College, etc. It has been distinctly announced that the position last accepted necessarily vacates the first one held. Is this provision now to be strictly enforced, and violations of it to be corrected by Executive authority, or is the law to be the servant of Executive power, and to execute its mandates only in such cases as may affect those who stand in the way of the will of the Governor?

The friends of nearly fifteen hundred patients who are now or have been under my charge, not one of whom could be found to testify aught against me, the hosts of approving and sympathizing citizens, eminent in every walk of life, whose kind expressions of gratification at my acquittal I am yet daily receiving, and the intelligent public, will not fail to put a just estimation upon the acts of an Executive that, lacking the courage to seek its hostile, personal and political ends by open means, resorts to indirection like this.

EUGENE GRISSOM.

ADDENDUM.

On the 22d August, 1889, the Board of Directors, as newly organized under R. H. Smith as President, accepted my resignation as Superintendent, tendered in the following terms, to take effect upon the election and qualification of a successor:

"*To the Board of Directors of the N. C. Insane Asylum:*

"GENTLEMEN:—Under the circumstances, I feel it my duty to tender my resignation of the office of Superintendent of the North Carolina Insane Asylum. Owing to the inability and consequent absence from duty of the Assistant Physician, my immediate departure would leave the institution without any medical care, and being unwilling to prejudice in the least degree the interests of the Asylum, it is agreeable to me, if it is the wish of the Board, to remain until my successor is appointed and installed, to whom it will afford me great pleasure to give full information respecting every detail of management, and in regard to every case in the Asylum, and to aid him in every way to enter upon the successful discharge of his duties.

"Very respectfully,

"EUGENE GRISSOM."

The following report was also presented, exhibiting the operations of the institution to date, since the last annual report:

"N. C. INSANE ASYLUM,
"RALEIGH, N. C., August 22d, 1889.

"*To the Board of Directors of the North Carolina Insane Asylum:*

"GENTLEMEN:—Upon retiring from the management of this institution it seems highly proper that I should make a statement of the workings and condition of this institution from December, 1888, the time of the last annual report, to this date, August 22d, 1889:

"Number under treatment December, 1888, 292; number admitted from December, 1888, to date, 67; whole number treated from December, 1888, to date, 359; number discharged from December, 1888, to date, 72; number now on the books, 287; number at home on probation and eloped, 6; total number now in the institution, 281. Number discharged as "cured," 46; number discharged as "improved," 6; number discharged as "unimproved," 1; number discharged as "died," 19; total number discharged, 72. Percentage of "cured" upon whole number admitted since December, 1888, 68.65; percentage of "deaths" upon whole number treated since December, 1888, 5.29.

"Reference to the above table will show the percentage of cured to be 68.65 and the death rate to be 5.29 per cent. for the last eight months and 22 days.

"The record speaks for itself, and the families of 46 afflicted restored to reason during that period rejoice in this noble charity and its achieved success.

"This is the largest percentage of cures during the history of this institution, and is not surpassed by any in the United States that receives and treats chronic insane. The mortality, though increased as it has been by several cases almost in the last stages of life when admitted, is still largely below the average of the institutions of the country.

"The endemic of catarrhal fever which prevailed in the female department has given unusual care and anxiety, but I am glad to say is apparently subsiding without as yet a single case of death, except one complicated with epilepsy of about twenty years' standing.

"My labors have been unusually onerous on account of the disability of the Assistant Physician since July 22d.

"In consequence of the arduous duties of the new Steward, in bringing up the books of the late Steward, some of which were several months behind, including the Classification Book and Ledger, I regret that I am not able to give you a detailed statement of the finances of the institution.

"On account of some complaints made by persons hauling wood to the institution, of the measurements upon which they were paid, and in order to find out whether these complaints were well founded, I ordered Mr. Crawford, the Steward, to make the statement which has been handed to the executive committee, and upon which there appears to be a deficiency of about 234 cords of wood paid for but not delivered, during the administration of the former Steward.

"Upon examination by the new Engineer important repairs have been found necessary to the gas-works and the water-works, which he seems to be executing with skill and dispatch. I herewith submit reports concerning his department.

"After twenty-one years of devoted service to the institution, I relinquish the trust with the assurance that it is in a better condition for the care and cure of the insane than ever heretofore, and with no abated interest in its future welfare.

"Very respectfully,

(Signed) "EUGENE GRISSOM,

"*Superintendent.*"

DR. GRISSOM'S REASONS FOR RESIGNING.

It is due to the people of the State whose institution this is, to the friends of justice and fair dealing, and to myself, to state some facts which prompted my resignation as Superintendent of the North Carolina Insane Asylum.

A long and patient investigation of many weeks was conducted to inquire into charges of unworthy conduct preferred against me by subordinate officers of the Asylum, and conceived in all the malice that characterizes men who conspire for evil ends, and permit no obstacles of truth or honesty to stand in the way of long cherished schemes of aggrandizement upon the ruin of others; aided by suborned testimony, in a prosecution bitter and violent in proportion as it was impotent and futile. I was acquitted of the vile charges by the Board of Directors who were intimately acquainted with my management of this Asylum for many years.

In spite of cunningly devised fables, and ingenious fabrications of stories of immorality; in spite of all that malice and envy and prejudice could do to distort the ordinary performance of duty in behalf of the insane into cruelty to their persons; in spite of ridiculous charges of peculation which fell almost still-born, as if from accusers conscious of their absurdity;—the eminent men who in a long series of years have given their time and sympathies to the insane rebuked the false witnesses and the malicious conspirators and their open and secret abettors, with a vote that was a complete endorsement of my official course, and a vindication of the purity and uprightness of the administration of this great charity.

This decision has been ratified by the action of the great number throughout our borders who have been or are personally connected with or interested in nearly fifteen hundred patients who have been under my charge, not one of whom could be induced to testify aught against me. But on the contrary, daily throughout the trial and to the present hour, I have received such testimonials of regard and sympathy, of indignant defence and hearty congratulation, that, coupled with the love of my patients now to be left, and the kind expressions from eminent and unprejudiced citizens everywhere, there is much to render retirement grateful. These things enable me to view with equanimity the efforts to injure me, of the wretched ingrates and the venal corruptionists who profit by their vindictiveness, to say nothing of the ignorant and misled, who will return in due time to the exercise of reason and fair judgment.

Crushed for a moment, by the judgment of the Board, upon the untruth and malice of their charges, the conspirators with their semi-political abettors rallied for another onslaught. Their family connections, those who profited by the large patronage of the Steward's office, those who saw something to gain in the general scramble for place upon a change of administration here, those whose excitable feelings could be stirred by tales of imaginary wrong, were gathered into so-called indignation meetings, held under the immediate influence of the abettors of the conspirators discredited by the action of the Board. Not one meeting of that character has taken place except under their engineering, with the possible exception of those at the homes of two members of the Board whose action is yet to be referred to.

These lawless proceedings were defended to the brink of anarchy, and the point of surrendering law and justice into the hands of the mob, by a sheet which seeks notoriety by slanderous scurrility, sacrificing manhood, truth and decency, in the search for sensations. By ingenious and persistent misrepresentation, false and misleading summaries of evidence which suppressed material points of the defence, and the utterance of long concealed hostility in villification of the management of the Asylum and myself, from a soul without conscience, a mind devoid of any conception of honor, and a pen without shame, the *State Chronicle* injected its venom into its fanatical followers, and even distorted the vision of journals of high character for truth and honesty, through the amazing assumption of its malicious assertions.

These preparations having been completed, a most extraordinary series of acts of Executive usurpation, and petty official tyranny, heretofore unparalleled in North Carolina, have taken place to arrange for the concluding scene of the drama. The political inspiration that accounts for the amazing audacity of these conspirators in attempting to mould a corrupt public sentiment, or the over-leaping ambition that sought to involve my friends in future political odium by exciting a wave of temporary public clamor through an ignorant and prejudiced press, reveals itself in the daring assumption of His Excellency, the Governor, to combine all the powers of government in his hands, heretofore ascribed to three co-ordinate branches of authority. He sets at defiance the Constitution, and usurps the power of the Legislature to appoint a Board of Public Charities, under the frivolous pretence that the power to appoint to a temporary vacancy in an unexpired term is a power to create a board which is expressly exempted from Executive appointment, and for the good reason that it was contemplated that this board of legislative appointment was to supervise the general conduct of all the boards acting by Executive authority.

This stretch of prerogative, done in the face of refusal by other Governors, to appoint a Board of Public Charities, although they recommended the Legislature to exercise its powers, is performed, on the face of it, to offer a courtesy to ward off the indignation of the friends of those members of the Board of Directors of the Asylum whose retirement from the board he had resolved to secure at all hazards.

Knowing full well that Dr. E. Burke Haywood was the Physician of the Deaf and Dumb, he yet re-appointed him in March, 1889, a Director of the Asylum, and it ought to have been known by him that Dr. Isaac Jackson was Superintendent of the Board of Health of Columbus county when he also appointed him as a Director of the Asylum in March last.

Has the Governor any legal authority to ask for the resignation of Directors? Certainly not, any more than any sheriff, or constable, or any other executive officer. There is a proper official of the judicial department of the government—the Attorney General—whose province it is by a suit of *quo warranto*, upon suitable proceedings before the authorized courts, to secure decisions on such questions.

Were it otherwise, we should see, as we beheld in this case, as barefaced a usurpation of all the powers of goverment as the most autocratic monarch dares to claim. In addition to this, all fair-minded men must be shocked by the indecency of the appointment to a position on the Board of Capt. Octavius Coke, the leader in the Legislature of 1877 of a prolonged and bitter partisan effort to remove me from office on account of political opinions cherished nine years previous, and before my entering upon this position, and of one known to be hostile to the judgment which had acquitted me. To this must be added the still more outrageous appointment of Thomas B. Womack, Esq., who has sought notoriety at this juncture by publicly denouncing me in a meeting of the character referred to, writing resolutions of a denunciatory character and publishing an article over his own signature, proposing a trick by which some newly constituted body might hold me accountable upon charges upon which I had already been tried and acquitted by such men as would have scorned to play the part of accuser and juryman, of prosecutor and judge, alternately, in the same case. To them are to be added two of the members who voted against me, and to sustain the infamous charges: Dr. Foote, who has been said for many years to have been seeking the position of Superintendent for himself, and Mr. Richard H. Smith, who has for months past been the ready recipient of slanders poured into his ears by the original conspirators in this case, or their tools. Other gentlemen were appointed upon this Board whose qualifications consist largely in their readiness to register the Executive will, having been unknown in public life hitherto. And then the Jacobin journal which is either the organ and mouth-piece of the Governor, or is for the time being the power behind which he is content to sail into the haven of imagined popularity, used the following language [August 16, 1889]:

"With a diplomacy worthy of an experienced diplomat, the Governor conceived the idea of securing the resignations of enough of the friends of Dr. Grissom on the Board to secure a change in its complexion. * * * Its significance is seen when we state that the Board as now constituted, instead of standing five to three in favor of Dr. Grissom's innocence, stands, as well as can be ascertained up to the hour of going to press, six to three in favor of his removal. * * * It is indeed fortunate for the State that at this important juncture we have as Chief Magistrate a man who had the nerve to do all in his power to secure the removal of Dr. Grissom."

The candor of this declaration is only equaled by its imbecility. This paper, which is apparently the organ of the Executive, informs members appointed on this Board that it is for the purpose of removing a man who has just been acquitted by as honorable men as North Carolina boasts; two of whom have been complimented by the Governor as he asked them to get out of his way.

Are honorable men to be insulted by asking them to go upon a jury, packed and instructed to convict? The history of the English race has not known that since the days of Titus Oates. Are judges to be appointed for the rehearing of a cause after acquittal; and is the condemnation of the accused to be settled beforehand? We have no parallel in our records later than Jeffreys, of immortal infamy. This is a proceeding worthy of Russian despotism, whose councils are ordered to condemn. But the freeborn Anglo-Saxon blood of North Carolinians must be kindled at this spectacle of petty tyranny, this wresting of a sacred oath "to *faithfully* execute the laws" by a sinister determination both to interpret and execute them to destroy one man, already triumphantly vindicated by men who would scorn to doff the cap to any petty Gesler.

The wolf said to the lamb, "I will eat you, for you muddied the brook." "No, for I am below, and you above." "But I must, for you muddied it last year." "Nay, I was not born then." "Yet again, I will destroy you, for your ancestors did." "You must go, Dr. Grissom, for you have been guilty of immorality." "No," says the Board of Directors of the Asylum, "it is not true." "You must go, for you have been guilty of cruelty." "No," say all the friends of all the patients who have been under his charge. "Yet you must and shall go, for twenty years ago you professed a different political faith from the Executive and you refuse to be his vassal to-day." So ends the tragic farce, for the present.

It would be folly indeed to ask for or expect anything but injury and embarrassment, to say nothing more, at the hands of a Board sent here to perform the play of my humiliation at the dictates of an Executive so regardless of law, decency or justice. I have therefore tendered my resignation to a Board of Directors under whom I would not serve, and who come with denunciations and the declared purpose to outrage me.

To the people of North Carolina, who may always be trusted to judge with uprightness, when the sober second thought has time to assert itself, I solemnly appeal against this high-handed tyranny of the State Executive, and, with patience, confidently await the verdict of popular vindication.

N. C. Insane Asylum, EUGENE GRISSOM.
Raleigh, August 23d, 1889.

www.ingramcontent.com/pod-product-compliance
Lightning Source LLC
Chambersburg PA
CBHW021643270326
41931CB00008B/1137

* 9 7 8 3 3 3 7 3 7 0 6 3 3 *